Where We Live

Japan

Donna Bailey and Anna Sproule

RSVP
RAINTREE
STECK-VAUGHN
P U B L I S H E R S
The Steck-Vaughn Company
Austin, Texas

Hello. My name is Reina.
I live in Tokyo, Japan.
Today I am wearing my best kimono,
which I only wear on special
holidays, like New Year's.

Tokyo is a very large, modern city.
It is the capital of Japan.
Tokyo has many buildings and cars,
and many people.

Most people in Tokyo live in apartments.
I live in these apartments with my parents
and my little brother Shota.
Our apartment is the one in the corner
on the top floor.

My school is close to our apartment.
I walk to school with my friend Eiko.
We carry our books and homework in
our red backpacks.

Everybody eats lunch at school.
We all sit together and eat
with our chopsticks.
My favorite lunch is fish and rice.

After lunch we play on the playground.
In the picture, you can see Yuka
balancing on a pair of "take uma."
They are stilts that raise
you high above the ground.

After school I often go
to the library with my friends.
I like books about different countries.
My little brother Shota chooses comics
because he likes the pictures.

Our apartment is small, so
on Sundays Mom and Dad often take us
to Yamashita Park for a picnic.
Many other families picnic
on the grass there, too.

One Sunday Mom took me and
my friends on a bus trip
to visit the Imperial Palace where
the Emperor of Japan lives.
The bridge in this picture leads to
the Imperial Palace.

There was another tour group there, too.
A photographer took pictures of them first,
and then he took pictures of us.
Our guide told us about the history
of Japan and the Emperor.

My friends and I bought funny masks
at the souvenir stands.
Do you know which mask I am wearing?

In the spring we go to
the kite festival at Hamamatsu.
The kites are huge and have many strings.
It takes a strong team of men
to control each kite.

I love spring because
it is cherry blossom time.
Families take picnics to the park
and sit under the cherry trees.

Women in kimonos give shows of
traditional Cherry Dances.
They wave their fans, and
people often join the dances.

15

People from offices bring their picnics
to the park, too.
They sing favorite songs in the sun
under the cherry trees.

One of my favorite holidays is New Year's Day.
Before the New Year starts, people hang
hundreds of red and white decorations
in the streets near my home.
Can you see the New Year decorations
in this picture?

At New Year's thousands of people
leave Tokyo and go to the country
to visit their grandparents.
My grandparents live in a mountain village
with rice fields all around it.

My mother, my brother Shota, and I
left Tokyo on December 27th
to avoid the heavy traffic.
My father owns a restaurant, so
he couldn't join us until New Year's Eve.

We went to the station and caught
the Bullet Train to the mountains.
It is the fastest train in Japan.
It travels at over 125 miles an hour.
It did not take long to get
to my grandparents' village.

When we arrived, we helped Grandfather
with the New Year decorations.
We bought the decorations at
a shop in the village.

Some people were also buying
rice cakes called "kagami-mochi."
To celebrate the new year, they put kagami-mochi
on the shrine as an offering to their god.

When Dad arrived from Tokyo, we made
our own kagami-mochi.
I helped him measure the rice and
knead the rice dough into round balls.

My grandparents have a small household
altar in the corner of their living room.
We decorated it with kagami-mochi, ferns,
braided straw, folded strips of paper,
and oranges to bring us luck.

Then I helped Grandfather decorate
a small altar in the garden with
kagami-mochi and strips of paper.

That evening Grandfather made a bonfire
of dead leaves and twigs in the yard.
He carefully raked the leaves into a pile.
When the fire was hot and glowing
in the middle, he showed Shota and me
how to roast sweet potatoes.

That night was New Year's Eve.
Mom and my grandmother helped me try on
the new kimono I would wear
on New Year's Day.
But Mom would not let me stay up until
midnight to welcome the New Year.

In the morning Shota and I opened
our New Year's presents.
I got a new purse, and Shota got an airplane.
Then we got dressed.
I wore my new kimono,
and Shota wore his new jacket.

28

We went with Grandfather to the shrine
to pray for good luck and happiness
for the coming year.

In the afternoon Dad took us
to the temple.
We did not need to wear
our best clothes then.

We watched the monks walk by
on their way to a New Year's service
in the great hall of the temple.
Everybody wished each other good luck
for the new year.

Afterward we walked around the temple.
Some shops sold candy, and others sold
books that tell your fortune.
I hope next year will be
a lucky one for me!

Index

Reading Consultant: Diana Bentley
Editorial Consultant: Donna Bailey
Supervising Editor: Kathleen Fitzgibbon

Illustrated by Sue Barclay/John Martin and Artists Ltd
Picture research by Suzanne Williams
Designed by Richard Garratt Design

Photographs:
Cover: Robert Harding Picture Library
All photographs by Bill Tingey except:
Robert Harding Picture Library: 1, 6, and 16
Library of Congress Cataloging-in-Publication Data: Bailey, Donna. Japan / Donna Bailey and Anna
Sproule. p. cm. —(Where we live)   SUMMARY: Text and pictures present life in Japan, particularly in its
capital city of Tokyo. ISBN 0-8114-2554-1 1. Japan—Social life and customs—1945– —Juvenile
literature. [1. Japan—Social life and customs. 2. Tokyo (Japan)—Social life and customs.] I. Sproule, Anna.
II. Title. III. Series: Bailey, Donna. Where we live. DS822.5.B35   1990   952′.135048—dc20
89-26093   CIP   AC

Trade Edition published 1992 © Steck-Vaughn Company

ISBN 0-8114-2554-1 hardcover library binding   ISBN 0-8114-7183-7 softcover binding

3 4 5 6 7 8 9 LB 96 95 94 93